FOR BETTE AND GENE—CA

IN MEMORY OF LEE WHEELOCK,
WHO TOLD ME I COULD—GN

Text is taken directly from Joseph Smith–History. The Publisher has provided chapter and
verse for all scripture, but has not indicated where ellipses have been used.

Illustrations © 2001 Wendy Winegar Bagley, Cary Austin, and Greg Newbold

Designed by Richard Erickson.

Bookcraft is a registered trademark of Deseret Book Company.

Visit us at www.deseretbook.com

ISBN 1-57345-908-9

Printed in the United States of America   42316-230

10 9 8 7 6 5 4 3

The First Vision

THE PROPHET JOSEPH SMITH'S
OWN ACCOUNT

ILLUSTRATIONS BY

CARY AUSTIN AND GREG NEWBOLD

BOOKCRAFT

Following a spiritual prompting, Joseph Smith went into the woods to pray. There he called upon God for wisdom and guidance. What followed was a singular spiritual experience that would change the course of humankind.

FOREWORD

 From the beginning, Heavenly Father planned that Joseph Smith would be the prophet of the Restoration. Throughout history, many prophets told of the time the gospel would be restored to the earth. One of those prophets was Joseph who was sold into Egypt. He prophesied that God would raise up a prophet who would also be named Joseph, after his father. Through him, God would bring his people to salvation.

That latter-day prophet was Joseph Smith. This is his own story of how it all began.

See 2 Nephi 3:6–16; Ephesians 1:4

I was born in the year of our Lord one thousand eight hundred and five, on the twenty-third day of December, in the town of Sharon, Windsor county, State of Vermont. My father, Joseph Smith, Sen., left the State of Vermont, and moved to Palmyra, Ontario when I was in my tenth year, or thereabouts. In about four years after my father's arrival in Palmyra, he moved with his family into Manchester in the same county of Ontario—

Joseph Smith–History 1:3

 Some time in the second year after our removal to Manchester, there was in the place where we lived an unusual excitement on the subject of religion. It became general among all the sects in that region of country. Indeed, the whole district of country seemed affected by it, and great multitudes united themselves to the different religious parties, which created no small stir and division amongst the people, some crying, "Lo, here!" and others, "Lo, there!"

Joseph Smith–History 1:5

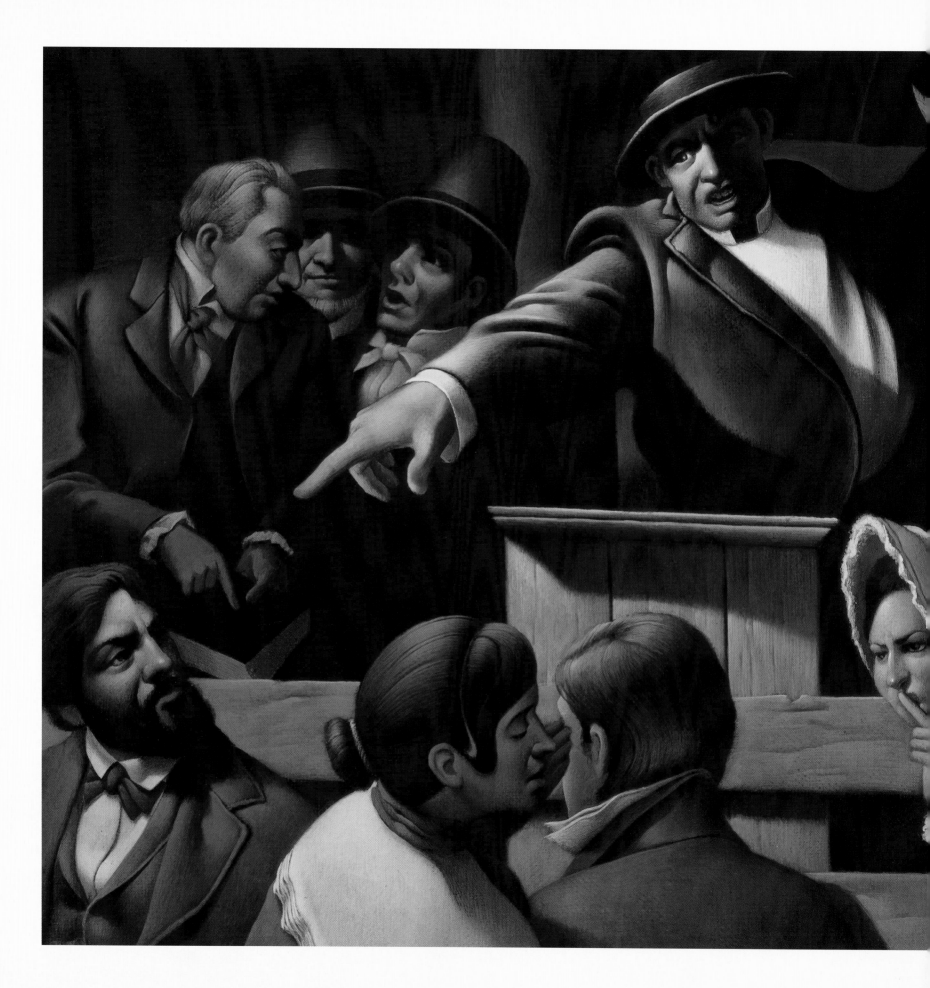

The respective clergy were active in getting up and promoting this extraordinary scene of religious feeling, in order to have everybody converted. Yet it was seen that the seemingly good feelings of both the priests and the converts were more pretended than real; for a scene of great confusion and bad feeling ensued— priest contending against priest, and convert against convert; so that all their good feelings one for another, if they ever had any, were entirely lost in a strife of words.

Joseph Smith–History 1:6

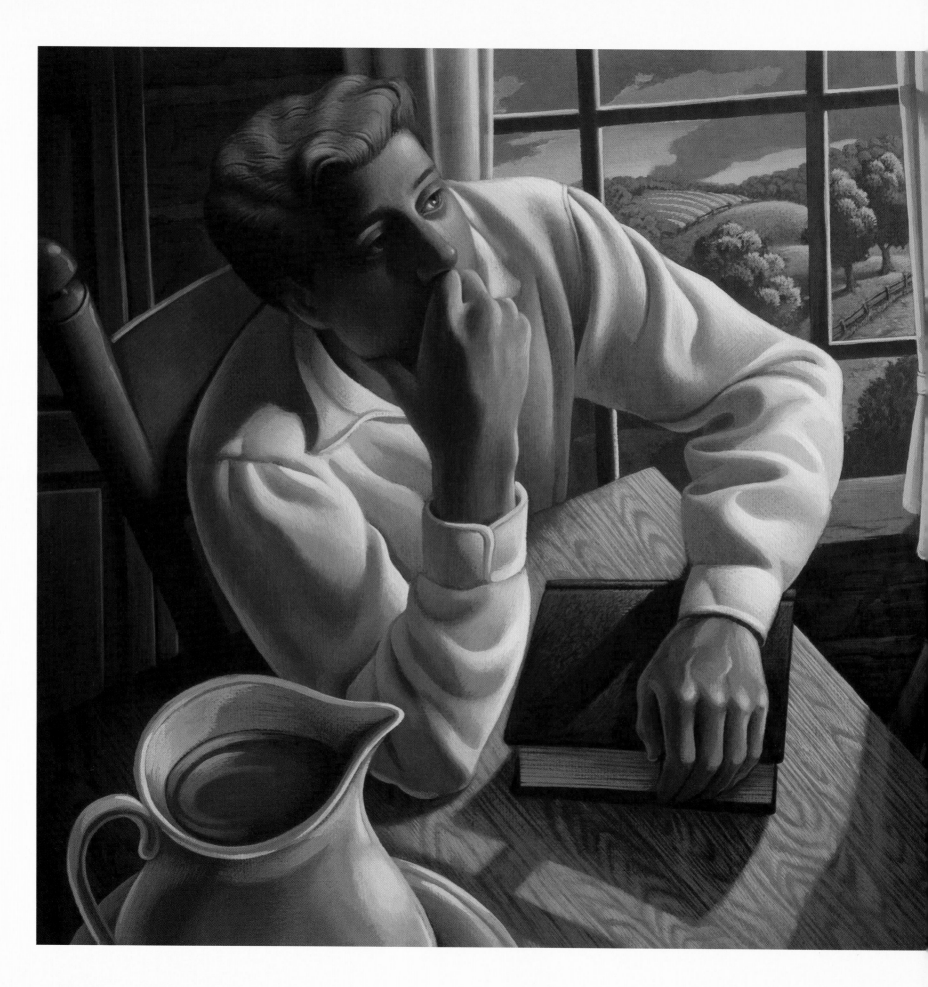

During this time of great excitement my mind was called up to serious reflection and great uneasiness; but though my feelings were deep and often poignant, still I kept myself aloof from all these parties. So great were the confusion and strife among the different denominations, that it was impossible for a person young as I was, and so unacquainted with men and things, to come to any certain conclusion who was right and who was wrong.

In the midst of this war of words and tumult of opinions, I often said to myself: What is to be done? Who of all these parties are right; or, are they all wrong together? If any one of them be right, which is it, and how shall I know it?

Joseph Smith–History 1:8, 10

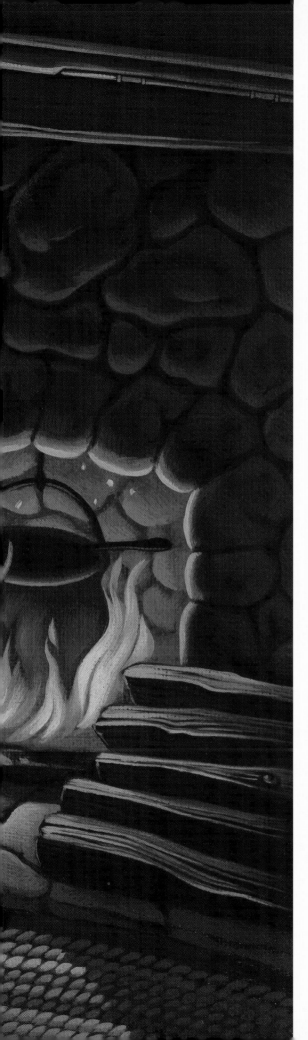

 While I was laboring under the extreme difficulties caused by the contests of these parties of religionists, I was one day reading the Epistle of James, first chapter and fifth verse, which reads: *If any of you lack wisdom, let him ask of God, that giveth to all men liberally, and upbraideth not; and it shall be given him.*

Never did any passage of scripture come with more power to the heart of man than this did at this time to mine. It seemed to enter with great force into every feeling of my heart. I reflected on it again and again, knowing that if any person needed wisdom from God, I did.

Joseph Smith—History 1:11–12

At length I came to the conclusion that I must either remain in darkness and confusion, or else I must do as James directs, that is, ask of God. I at length came to the determination to "ask of God," concluding that if he gave wisdom to them that lacked wisdom, and would give liberally, and not upbraid, I might venture.

So, in accordance with this, my determination to ask of God, I retired to the woods to make the attempt.

Joseph Smith—History 1:13–14

It was on the morning of a beautiful, clear day, early in the spring of eighteen hundred and twenty. It was the first time in my life that I had made such an attempt, for amidst all my anxieties I had never as yet made the attempt to pray vocally.

After I had retired to the place where I had previously designed to go, having looked around me, and finding myself alone, I kneeled down and began to offer up the desires of my heart to God.

Joseph Smith–History 1:14–15

I had scarcely done so, when immediately I was seized upon by some power which entirely overcame me, and had such an astonishing influence over me as to bind my tongue so that I could not speak. Thick darkness gathered around me, and it seemed to me for a time as if I were doomed to sudden destruction.

Joseph Smith–History 1:15

At the very moment when I
was ready to sink into despair
and abandon myself to
destruction—I saw a pillar of
light exactly over my head,
above the brightness of the
sun, which descended gradually until it fell upon me.
It no sooner appeared than I found myself
delivered from the enemy which held me bound.

Joseph Smith–History 1:16–17
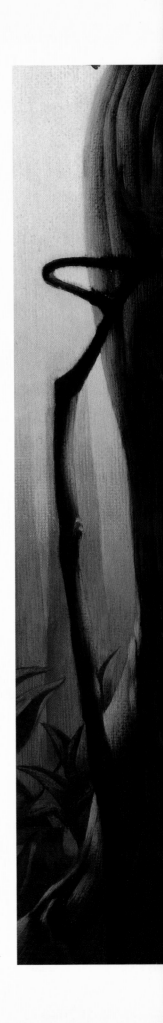

When the light rested upon me I saw two Personages, whose brightness and glory defy all description, standing above me in the air. One of them spake unto me, calling me by name and said, pointing to the other—*This is My Beloved Son. Hear Him!*

No sooner did I get possession of myself, so as to be able to speak, than I asked the Personages who stood above me in the light, which of all the sects was right and which I should join.

I was answered that I must join none of them, for they were all wrong: and all their creeds were an abomination; that those professors were all corrupt; that: "they draw near to me with their lips, but their hearts are far from me, they teach for doctrines the commandments of men, having a form of godliness, but they deny the power thereof."

Joseph Smith–History 1:17–19

When I came to myself again, I found myself lying on my back, looking up into heaven. When the light had departed, I had no strength; but soon recovering in some degree, I went home.

I had seen a vision; I knew it, and I knew that God knew it, and I could not deny it.

I had found the testimony of James to be true—that a man who lacked wisdom might ask of God, and obtain, and not be upbraided.

Joseph Smith–History 1:20, 25, 26

Afterword

 Joseph Smith's first vision was the beginning of a series of events that led him to be the first prophet of The Church of Jesus Christ of Latter-day Saints. Through him, Heavenly Father and Jesus Christ gave to earth the lost truths of the gospel.

Joseph spent his life serving the Church. On June 27, 1844, he died for the gospel's sake. As Joseph of Egypt had foretold, Joseph Smith was the prophet whom the Lord raised up to bring truth and salvation to His people.